Hind end'sight

Cathy Nelson

WestBow
PRESS
A DIVISION OF THOMAS NELSON

WestBow Press books may be ordered through booksellers or by contacting:

WestBow Press
A Division of Thomas Nelson
1663 Liberty Drive
Bloomington, IN 47403
www.westbowpress.com
1-(866) 928-1240

ISBN: 978-1-4497-8977-0 (sc)
ISBN: 978-1-4497-8978-7 (e)
Library of Congress Control Number: 2013905838

Edited by Sue Miholer: Picky, Picky Ink .

Printed in the United States of America.

WestBow Press rev. date: 4/5/2013

Table of Contents

And the glory goes to God.

Illustrations

by my beautiful grandchildren

Paul

Meraiah

Ezra

Jacob

Simon

and

Bethany

You hold my heart

Dedication

To my loving husband whose encouragement kept me writing.

To my loving son and daughter-in-law whose walk with the Lord is true.

To my loving God I dedicate my all.

Preamble

Learning about God should be joyous.

It should not be drudgery.

When did our hearts become so hardened?

Today, if you hear his voice,
do not harden your hearts.
Hebrews 3:15

Chapter 1

Rocks look better when wet

*The L*ORD *does not look at the things people look at.*
People look at the outward appearance,
*but the L*ORD *looks at the heart.*
1 Samuel 16:7

Cathy Nelson

*T*HEY CALL THEMSELVES CHRISTIANS. WHY WOULD I *want to be one? Why would I want to be like them? They say if I become one, it will change my heart. I will be born again. I don't see that in them. They walk around with a "holier than thou" attitude, yet look how rude they just were to that waitress. They didn't even apologize.*

They keep trying to cram their beliefs down my throat, using words like sinner, judgment, atonement, and blasphemy. They are a bunch of hypocrites. "Do as I say, not as I do." They act as if they understand everything yet when I ask a simple question, they stumble over their answer.

What has Jesus done for them that common sense hasn't already done for me? They don't have anything over me. They are not more intelligent. They aren't any nicer. I try to be a good person. I think that counts for something. Doesn't it? I don't think God has a problem with that.

What have I got to gain by becoming a Christian? I don't want to be changed if it means I will be like them. I don't want to buy what they are selling. Their advertising method makes me want to run in the opposite direction. They are so legalistic yet they break all their own rules. Don't they see what I see?

MY GRANDFATHER WAS AN AMATEUR ROCK hound. He dug dusty ugly rocks from the earth and ran water over them to reveal their hidden beauty. Then he would put them in a tumbler to spin and they would emerge polished and smooth as glass. Pretty as candy. Flawless it seemed. Perfect.

How could he have known which rocks to pick? How did he recognize them from all the "look-alikes" lying side by side in the dust?

How I treasured those miracle rocks he gave me. To this day, I keep those special rocks in my jewelry box. Indeed, they are more precious to me than the jewelry next to them.

As a small child, I assumed the miracle was in the rocks. Was it, or was Grandpa just able to recognize the potential within them? Did he simply possess the patience to work with the rocks until he produced a beautiful metamorphosis in them?

Are we not just like those rocks? Do we not have the potential to shine? How will that happen? Can anyone see our potential? Can we see it? Do we even know what our potential is? God sees it and He loves us before we reach it. But can we reach it on our own?

Our character can appear gray and dusty—badly in need of a bold spray of water to rinse away our crusty exterior.

This may not be enough. God may have to tumble us around for awhile before our best can be revealed. Tumble until we are polished smooth. Sometimes He may need to pull us out of the tumbler, test us a bit and then put us back in for another tumble.

You know what I'm talking about. We are all dusty. Ever yell at the crazy driver who just cut you off in traffic? Or what about the poor salesperson who had nothing to do with the expiration date on your coupon? How about the telemarketer over the phone? Ouch! That one hit home, didn't it? I know it did for me.

Dust is flying, isn't it? Ever feel like you are two people? First, the one who controls your mouth, and second, the real you. Yeah, the one who controls your heart. The one under all the dust. The one who at times may not be very visible. The one who longs to bust out of the dirt clod and just shine.

We all want to be that person. Not just some of the time but twenty-four hours a day. So why is it that it seems so hard to achieve? Why is it that sometimes we catch ourselves acting as if a dump truck just backed up and dropped its load all over our head? Maybe because it is so easy to mistake ourselves for someone we are not.

The last time we looked in the mirror we were shining. I came. I tumbled. I shine. I know Jesus. I'm saved. I have arrived. I learned that lesson. I'm born again. I can move on. I can sit back and watch all those poor dusty souls who haven't been polished yet and feel a bit smug.

Watch out! Smug is pretty close to the word smudged. Smudged is definitely not polished.

Repeat after me:

Christian rocks are no better than other rocks!

Christian rocks are no better than other rocks!

We are all sinners. We all do and say dumb things. Even when we are working on improving ourselves. And our dust is more than skin deep. That is precisely why we need Jesus. Polishing us is a really big job. "BIG." We can't do it alone. We can't do it in our own power. Jesus sees our potential and He is big enough for the job.

It is not about what we do. It is about what He does.

"But God demonstrates his own love for us in this: While we were still sinners, Christ died for us. Since we have now been justified by his blood, how much more shall we be saved from God's wrath through him!" (Romans 5:8-9).

But it is not until we go to be with Him that we will be made like Him. Until then we struggle and we must keep our eyes fixed on Him and continue working toward that goal. The mature Christian understands that they he or she is sinful and that they have a need for ongoing spiritual restoration. But a word to devout Christians everywhere (and I include myself in this): Where is your *joy*? He asks for devout not dour. Commitment calls for a true relationship and in the relationship lies the *joy*. Does your face reflect *joy?*

We are not better. The difference is that we acknowledge it, ask for help from our Savior Jesus Christ, by His grace are forgiven, and are promised a place with Him for eternity.

So we need to be working Christians. Ever striving to follow God's will. It is not enough to say we believe. He calls for a deep change in us. He places a desire in our hearts to work out our salvation. When we build a relationship with Him—reading, praying, and learning from His word, asking Him to guide our actions—then we begin to understand our role. It is not about strict man made rules. It is about our identity with Christ.

We learn that it isn't about appearances that are so hard to sustain, but rather, it is about a true change of heart. Coming to Him with a humble attitude and a willingness to give up our false sense of control and watch the Master at work.

When we allow God to polish our character, He works through our granite exterior to the core. He polishes us from the inside, out. A polish that will endure the ages.

So, the next time someone tells you that they think you are "all wet," remember the tumbler and graciously answer, "Thank you; I'm working on it."

We are all beginners, and sometimes it is necessary to begin again.

*Today, if you hear his voice,
do not harden your hearts.*
Hebrews 3:15

Chapter 2

Truth and other uncertainties

For the foolishness of God is wiser than human wisdom, and the weakness of God is stronger than human strength.
1 Corinthians 1:25

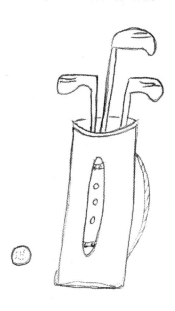

Cathy Nelson

THE GAME OF GOLF DOESN'T MAKE a lot of sense. I learned to play years after I had mastered many other sports. Sports like volleyball and baseball. They came easy to me. I felt like I was a natural athlete. Be strong; hit hard. That always worked for me. No problem.

Then came golf. I had a lot to learn.

"What do you mean, I don't want to smack the ball? Of course I do. I want it to fly down that fairway. *Watch*; I'll show you. Like this; *oops!* Why didn't it fly? You saw me. You saw the power. Why didn't it go sailing?"

My instructor explains: "You have to let the club do the work."

Yes, yes, of course I do, but let me just show you how I'm gonna power it down the fairway this time. Here we go; watch this; *oops!* Why didn't it fly? I can hit it harder than all the other students combined. Seriously, the way I hit that ball, it should be in the next county by now. What's going on?

My instructor again patiently explains: "You have to let the club do the work."

Well that doesn't make much sense. If I want it to go far, I'm going to need to put some muscle behind it.

Again and again he explains: "You are going to have to

trust the club." It's all in the technique. Your grip, posture, stance. It is about accuracy. Try a slower swing.

Are you nuts? A slower swing? Everyone knows a slower swing will result in less distance. Why, that just goes against the laws of nature. I'm out here to put some distance on this thing. That's crazy! *Trust the club; slower swing.*

OK, OK. I'll swing slower, but only to show you that it doesn't make any sense. Here we go … I can't do it. I really can't. It's just too hard! A swing is a swing. My arm just goes fast naturally. This is against everything I know." *Try again; trust the club.*

OK, slowwwww … swinggggg …

OH … MY … HEAVENS …

"Did you see that ball fly? Did you see how far it went? Really—the club did that? I just let the club do the work! I can't believe it! The club did that?" *Trust; let the club do the work.*

We expect this of God also. We want God in a single lesson plan. We want everything about Him to make sense, right now. We want it all to be black and white. Easy-care instructions. Simple to understand. We want Him to follow our idea of what makes sense, and when He refuses to be that small, we dismiss the whole idea as silly. Something for lesser people.

When He asks us to think outside the box, we refuse. Instead, we want Him to get inside the box. We want Him to be domestic, tame. Mostly we just want Him on our terms. If He refuses to be our genie and grant us our every wish, we really just don't know what to do with Him. So we do nothing with Him. We deny Him. If it initially doesn't follow our reason, then we don't follow Him.

"As the heavens are higher than the earth, so are my ways higher than your ways and my thoughts than your thoughts" (Isaiah 55:9).

He didn't promise it would be easy. He said the path was narrow. He surely didn't say He would follow our rules. As a matter of fact, sometimes what He does say sounds a bit crazy to us. But remember: It doesn't come from our mind. It comes from His. It doesn't follow our understanding. It follows truth. He is truth.

"Trust; let God do the work."

Is there such a thing as truth?

Certainty is arrogant and therefore wrong. Why? Because somebody said so? We pride ourselves on being smart, enlightened, politically correct, and tolerant. We, however, are not tolerant of only one truth. We worry to the extreme about offending others until we can no longer see clearly that a truth exists. We don't want to appear arrogant, but is truth arrogant?

Truth, by definition, is exclusive. It is impossible for everything to fall under truth. It naturally excludes all else. We must decide what is true. If we choose to not "rock the boat" over truth, we have denied truth for the sake of our comfort. If the wind is blowing, it is true. If the sun is shining, it is true. It's a kind of "Trick or Treat." We are tricked or we are treated by the truth.

"Jesus answered, 'I am the way and the truth and the life'" (John 14:6).

Trust; let God do the work.

He has created in us a desire to know the truth. A desire to search for the truth. To assist us, He has installed a moral compass that points to the truth. Why are we so quick to make excuses for our bad behavior? It is our internal compass that points to the truth and quietly calls us. "Come. Don't go in that direction. Don't behave that way." Our internal compass. It is not our feelings or emotion. It is not our heart. The heart is a pump. It is our soul. The soul is a compass. It knows the way home.

Why do we call life sacred? Why do we do everything to uphold that? Because life is sacred and it isn't a coincidence. Life has meaning. **To follow the Truth**.

To follow the truth through good and bad until we understand the truth. To persevere until it does make sense. The Lord is truth and our soul's compass is set to Him. All life is sacred because all life is His.

Trust: *Let God do the work.*

My employment is in the medical field. I once worked with an Alzheimer's patient who could rarely speak a complete sentence correctly. Yet, without fail, when asked to say a prayer, she would recite one—without a single error in grammar. Chance? Or a very intelligent, powerful force at work. It doesn't make sense—or does it?

You can read plenty of books that will educate you on the historic evidence for the Bible's teaching. You can and should use all your mind and reasoning to decide what you believe. There is proof, but proof will never stand alone. If you are using all the logic of Spock from Star Trek, it will not be enough. It will never be enough. You must also use what has been planted in you. Listen to the wisdom planted in your soul. Deep where your faith lies. Your compass.

When my five-year-old granddaughter was asked: "Can you read?" she thought a moment and then answered boldly: "No, but I can tell what the words say by the letters."

Perhaps this is where scientists fall short today. Perhaps they are so focused on trying to read the universe that they neglect to see the letters. Many theories have been discovered–good and worthwhile pursuits, all. To name a few: Einstein's theory of relativity, quantum theory, gravity, and string theory. Read about them. They are fascinating, but they are incomplete.

The universe is interconnected, but the theories aren't. They haven't been unified. Try as they might, the scientists can't unify them. There is something missing that these highly trained and intelligent individuals can't understand. What is it?

This must be amusing to the Lord. Because perhaps they are so busy "reading" the universe that they forgot to look at the letters. The letters are G-O-D. Praise the day when they discover it is He who unifies everything.

"If from there you seek the LORD your God, you will find him if you seek him with all your heart and with all your soul" (Deuteronomy 4:29).

God reveals when you seek Him in earnest.

For some time, I felt a greater dignity in remaining quiet about my spirituality. I had witnessed so many others open their mouths and mess it all up. I was embarrassed because I couldn't answer all the questions. I felt that

I would fall short. Then I realized that I didn't have to know everything. I couldn't know everything. This was a relationship with a much taller intelligence and I am short.

When I was a child and my mother told me the stove was hot, I trusted. I wasn't following blind. I was learning. I could get close to the stove and feel the heat and realize she was correct. The stove was hot. I could trust her.

Look around you. Really look and listen. Watch a sunset. Go to a nursery room and look at the beautiful row of babies. Learn the many ways a body heals itself. Look at the leaves bud out on the trees in spring. Listen to your soul's compass and hear what it declares. God has revealed enough to us so that we know we can trust Him.

Trust; let God do the work.

"Ask and it will be given to you; seek and you will find; knock and the door will be opened to you" (Matthew 7:7).

Faith is a decision, not an emotion. When our emotions come into play, we will at times be uncertain. If we are hurting, we may doubt God cares or that He is there for us. We want things to go our way. We want to be masters of our own fate, and when things don't go our way, we may question our faith. Don't go with your emotional doubts.

You don't come to know God and then, with the swipe of a magic wand, suddenly understand everything. We can start with faith the size of a mustard seed. (See Matthew 17:20.) God accepts uncertainty, if it asks for truth. We don't have to have *all* the answers to have *the* answer.

The path of spiritual growth is a path of lifelong learning. The good news is: The act of being uncertain does not alter truth. It is never too late. We do not need to be embarrassed about our age. God does not call us all at the same age or time. This may be your time. Open your mind, open your Bible and wait on the Lord. He continues to teach.

"Once more I will shake not only the earth but also the heavens. The words 'once more' indicate the removing of what can be shaken—that is, created things—so that what cannot be shaken may remain" (Hebrews 12:26–27).

Christianity has endured by His design. It cannot be shaken.

When playing through the game of golf, let the club do the work. But when working through life let God do the work.

Today, if you hear his voice,
do not harden your hearts.
Hebrews 3:15

Chapter 3

Stop sign ... turn green

I raised you up for this very purpose,
that I might display my power in you and
that my name might be proclaimed in all the earth.
Romans 9:17

WHEN MY SON WAS ABOUT THREE years old, he was riding in his car seat in the back of the car as I pulled up to a stop sign. There were no cars in any direction, so I accelerated and continued on my way down the road. Suddenly, this small, reprimanding voice from the back seat declares, "Mom, the stop sign didn't turn green yet. Why did you go?"

"What!"

"The stop sign was red, Mom, when you started going!"

Ahhh! Well, I had to explain the difference between stoplights and stop signs. "One turns green, while the other leaves it up to us to determine when it is safe to go." That was a very cherished moment for me. He will never remember that moment, and I will never forget it.

Reflecting on that now, it occurs to me that as adults we are a little like that. We want all of life to have very clear direction. We want everything to point to one clear purpose. A purpose that will satisfy our every reason for existence. A very grand "ONE BIG THING" that will define us as unique from all others.

We want this purpose to be clear so we will have no doubt when we have reached it. We imagine that once we have fulfilled this purpose, we will sit back and have a huge sense of accomplishment—a feeling that "I have done what I was born to do!"

But, what if the stop sign doesn't turn green. What if we spend our lives searching and trying, yet never feel we did any grand thing. We have heard from many people that we need to find a purpose for our lives. What is wrong with us if we don't find it? Are we not trying hard enough? Are we lazy, or do we have some kind of defect that makes us pretty much worthless?

Some people seem to know early in their lives, stay the course for years, and even become famous for their big contribution that changed the world. This is a good thing—and more power to them! We need them all. However, let us think about God's Word on this a moment:

"For it is God who works in you to will and to act in order to fulfill his good purpose" (Philippians 2:13).

What did that say? Could it be that it is not for our purpose that we strive and toil? Could it be that it is not for our purpose that we are placed here? It says: "to will and to act in order to fulfill his good purpose." His good purpose encompasses much more than ours ever could. It is vast and far-reaching, and it is not just one large one. It involves purpose after tiny purpose all interconnected for eternity. Now, that is an accomplishment! The passage goes on to say:

"Do everything without grumbling or arguing, so that you may become blameless and pure, 'children of God without fault in a warped and crooked generation.' Then you will shine among them like stars in the sky" (Philippians 2:14–15).

He is asking us to accept what we are doing with a gracious heart because it all has value and purpose. When we do this, we will shine like stars in the universe. That sounds pretty grand to me. Sign me up for that purpose. Wait! There's more. It turns out there is also clear direction for our part in this. He gives us direction in His Word if we will just read it. When we are serving Him and His purpose, He will give us the power to do it. Read on.

"I raised you up for this very purpose, that I might display my power in you and that my name might be proclaimed in all the earth" (Romans 9:17).

He will display His power in us. We are not worthless or lazy. We will be powered by Him. We will shine like stars in the universe and we will proclaim His name in all the earth.

His purpose; His clear direction.

We are not common. We are made holy through Him and this is to be our clear direction.

I have witnessed people say, "I couldn't really do anything much, so I didn't do anything at all." I have said this. We all have. The bee takes pollen from one flower at a time and moves it to another and another. Slowly, carefully, day after day, until the fields explode with God's beautiful glory. We don't need great abilities. We just need to show up in all the tiny moments. Reach out and touch all that is close enough to touch.

Mother Teresa said, "We are called to make a difference in the places that we are." Look for what you are passionate about. Pursue it, by all means; but stop choking on the fact that you haven't done something huge. Many small things often grow into big things.

Our humanity toward one another displays God's love. My place is to care for sick and often dying patients. When a person is dying, it becomes ever so clear that they would like our expert care, but they desire our humanity. A touch from a caring hand, an understanding ear, a whispered prayer. These are what they desire. This becomes our purpose. The moments. Find your purpose in the moments.

I was walking a patient down the hall of the hospital one evening. She was a woman in her forties. Not young, not old. She had a hurdle ahead of her. Surgery and a serious illness to overcome. She surprised me by suddenly turning to me and asking if I knew how to pray.

It felt odd to me that someone would feel prayer was something that had to be learned. Where did she get that idea? From Christians? Do we use such fancy words and protocol that we alienate those that would follow, if only it didn't seem so complicated? I simply answered, "Yes. Would you like me to pray with you?" She would.

I prayed in language as simple as I could, willing her to understand that God wants the heart, not the showy words.

When I was finished, she hugged me and said, "Now I know there is a God because He sent me you."

I told her, "He is here. He is in everything. He is yours, if you want Him."

This moment and many like it rush by us. Some lost forever because we see them as too small to pursue. I pray we will not make the mistake of thinking we will pursue Jesus after we finish this job or complete that task or after we have found our single illusive purpose.

God is your purpose because His purpose is yours. He is the center of everything. Colossians tells us all things were created by Him and for Him. He is before all things and in Him all things hold together.

Time with God should take place in all activities. Each can serve Him in some small way. You may not be famous, but you will be right where God wants you. Every year, every day, every moment holds your purpose.

The stop sign is green … Go!

*Today, if you hear his voice,
do not harden your hearts.*
Hebrews 3:15

Chapter 4

The human race

Stop and consider God's wonders.
Job 37:14

I WAS JOGGING UP A HILL IN the early morning cold. A fog bank crept silently behind me. A heavy dampness crowded near. I could hear my heart beat louder. My initial reaction was to run faster. Stay ahead of it. I shouldn't let it overtake me. I could already feel some of its effects. My hair hung in wet strands around my face. "Run faster," I whispered to myself.

But then, without warning, it enveloped me. Reached with its thick silent arms and encircled me. It caressed my limbs, my face. I felt as if it was accepting me as part of its whole. Including me as one with its nature. I was hidden and protected from all the noisy world. I liked it. Why had I wanted to escape from its comforting embrace, its protective silence? As a child, I had loved the fog. Loved its mystery. What have I forgotten? Am I too old for its simple joy? What am I racing against?

Are you racing against something or racing in pursuit of something? What is it? Do you know? Do you understand why or what you pursue?

Many of us are looking for happiness in department stores and real estate offices. This hunt requires much time and effort with mostly poor results. We seem to be trading more possessions for less value and it requires us to work harder at making a living—and work less at making a life. Where is the finish line to your race? Are you forfeiting eternal rewards for temporary benefits here on earth?

Somewhere along the line, our culture has evolved from working just enough to support our families, into a "never stop, we need more" attitude. We must earn more, but at what expense? What is it we strive for? Do we already have it? If we slowed down, could we see it through the fog? Do we need more stuff or does our stuff need more stuff?

Next time you stand in a crowded elevator, notice what happens. Does everyone suddenly take up a study on shoes? Does anyone look you in the face and smile? If someone catches you looking at them, do they look away embarrassed? When did this happen? Perhaps when we all joined the "race." We became too busy to strike up a conversation and then, unpracticed, we simply became bad at it. Now, put a child in the same elevator. Is he afraid to talk? Are you more likely to speak to him? Is that because we intuitively know that the child will be more open to our conversation? Could this be because children are not yet in the race?

It is time to reclaim the passion of the moment. Slow down. Is first always best? Is busiest always better? Even in serving we can overdo. Many Christians believe that we must serve day and night—that no other activity is worthy. They feel continually guilty that they are not doing enough. Are we serving or just busy? Are we sharing love or trying to impress ourselves or others? Are we feeding our soul or our ego? We should question our intentions. We should not rejoice in our pride.

Is productivity so important? When our computers go down, we can't do anything. It's called "downtime." It's all a waste. Unless we can hit the refresh button and bring it up again. What about a human refresh button? Maybe a little reprogramming is in order.

Many financial analysts will tell us we need to work harder and longer to plan for retirement. They lay out figures that sometimes astound me. Don't get me wrong! I am a planner. I believe in having a plan and working toward its goal, but what are we planning for?

What do we need to be happy? What is the real treasure at the finish line? What is it we want to find at the end of the race? If we focus all our energy on what we don't yet have, there will be no energy left for all that we do have—today, in this moment.

Stand still. You need not go any further to find happiness. It will not come once you are married. It will not come after you purchase that new house or with your next promotion at work. Don't wait for these things to make you happy. In this quiet moment, happiness lies waiting for you. Halt, and let it settle around you.

Next time you ask someone how they're doing, stop, look them in the eyes, and wait on their answer. Connect with them; hear what they have to say. God put them in front of you. This is one of those "purpose moments." Consider its importance. Circle around it.

When we want to eat, we must take the time to prepare the meal, but it is not all preparing. Some of it is eating. Enjoy the food. God wants us to take the time to nourish one another in this way.

If we pile one activity on top of another in our schedule, we will get to the point where we can't effectively do any of it. This is only going through the motions. It is not serving well, and at this speed, we will miss the blessings in the serving. Be courageous, learn from a child. Play is not frivolous. Remember the simple things of your childhood—long before you joined the race.

Let's slow our pace. Look back! Allow all that is good to catch up to us. We may have passed the road to the finish line without even knowing. Look closely through the fog of this world. You may discover something wonderful waiting there. You may discover today's portion of joy.

Now, with the fog all around me, I turn and run straight into the thickest part of the cloud bank. Layer upon layer, growing denser. I can barely make out the path ahead. I am forced to slow my steps. Moisture runs down my nose and drips off the tip. I laugh and stick my tongue out to catch the droplets. I don't need to race against the fog bank. I need to be a sponge and absorb the fog. I want to absorb all the treasure God offers in this life.

*Today, if you hear his voice,
do not harden your hearts.*
Hebrews 3:15

Chapter 5

The cookie crumbles

My grace is sufficient for you,
for my power is made perfect in weakness.
2 Corinthians 12:9

Cathy Nelson

W HEN MY SON WAS ABOUT FIVE years old, he was listening to me comment about an event that should have occurred, but didn't. He studiously attempted to verbalize the quote he had heard me use many times in the past. It came out of his mouth: "Well, Mom, that is just the way the cookie falls apart."

Almost accurate and very cute! And so, my son was well on his way to becoming the kind of man who could pour the milk to enjoy with the cookie, whole or in pieces—no matter, how it came to him from the cookie jar of life.

What do you do when your cookie falls apart? Unexpected crumbs fall through your fingers and down the inside of your shirt. Do you go after them, frantically stuffing each tidbit into your mouth as quickly as possible so you can go after the many other pieces?

What if it's a chocolate chip cookie? Now you have chocolate smears on your clothes that only spread further as you try to pick them off. What is your attitude as you attempt to bring order back to your snacking? *Didn't your mother teach you not to talk with your mouth full?* It might even be possible that as you overreact, you bump your glass of milk off the table and send it sailing in puddles to the four corners of the room.

What are our choices here?

1. Become very upset; let it overwhelm you; cease to function.

2. Ask for God's wisdom and calmly begin the cleanup.

3. Throw your head back in laughter and reach for another cookie.

Truthfully most of us would probably react with some combination of the three and you may be thinking: *Is this cookie crisis really big enough to warrant all this contemplation?* Maybe not. However, life consists of many crumbly events. Many of them unforeseen. How we react to those events plays a huge role in how we perceive our happiness level. This brings us to the question: Is life fair?

Not when you wash your car and it doesn't even rain, but then someone rear-ends you on the way home. Or when the mechanic tells you that your car needs only a small part. The cost is just $5.99; however, the labor will be $999.00. OK! I know we are talking about serious trials here. Financial troubles, failed marriages, poor health, and job loss. These things can be truly overwhelming. Is life unfair?

"Everyone comes naked from their mother's womb, and as everyone comes, so they depart. They take nothing from their toil that they can carry in their hands" (Ecclesiastes 5:15).

What does this mean? You come into this world with nothing, and you are going out with nothing, so deal with it! Yes!

Or wait. It says, "Nothing from their toil that they can carry in their hands." Perhaps our riches are not the tangible things. Perhaps, they truly are the things unseen.

Remember when you were a child and there was at least one kid on the block whose parents let them do almost anything they wanted? You were always whining to your parents: "Johnny can ride his bike to the other side of the railroad tracks. Why can't I?" Inevitably, their answer was: "Because I said so." But, what was behind all those "I said so's"? Love. They knew far better than we did just what was good for us. However, they may not have always revealed their reasons.

We had to learn that lesson as children, and we need to learn it all over again as God's children. God loves us. He desires to bring His children to perfection, in preparation for the day we join Him at our permanent address.

"Yet to all who did receive him, to those who believed in his name, he gave the right to become children of God" (John 1:12).

He may not reveal His reasons immediately, but He wants us to learn to rely on Him—not on ourselves—as we seem to think we can. Sometimes we must get to a desperate place, before we understand this fully. G. Campbell Morgan wrote: "Inevitably, sooner or later there comes a crisis in which we are brought to the appalling sense of our own weakness. That is a great hour."

Sometimes it is necessary that we get to a place where we feel helpless before we will accept His help. Alone, we are helpless. Does His offer of help suddenly sound better?

Remember, we were not put on this earth to achieve our purpose. We are here to achieve His purpose. This is why He created us. Sometimes, affliction accomplishes His purpose. We want to think that if we are good people, God will spare us all the suffering and simply reward us. He will reward us. He will see that justice prevails. In His own time. Not in ours.

"No eye has seen, ...no ear has heard, ... no human mind has conceived—the things God has prepared for those who love him" (1 Corinthians 2:9).

God does not follow our theology or plan. We cannot begin to guess His next move or His reason for it. He is beyond our limited comprehension. He doesn't think like us nor does He keep score like we attempt to do. His perspective on fairness is totally different than ours, but He knows us intimately.

Children of God, we are the lucky ones. Our childhood on this earth will know hardship, but He will help us walk through the hardship without being devastated. We may bear a bigger burden than some. It may seem unfair. We may watch others get away with—well yes, even murder—but God will give us the grace to endure. And when we grow up and rest beside the Lord, we will see clearly the splendid fairness that is far too distant for us to grasp today.

We will have our questions answered. We will find our new home well worth the journey. We shall have our reward. We shall lack nothing. Our future is certain and God is our Father.

"I consider that our present sufferings are not worth comparing with the glory that will be revealed in us" (Romans 8:18).

Perhaps we should throw the word "fair" out of our vocabulary. God speaks beyond the rules and rituals we have been living by. He will give us an ordinary life with duties and comfort, with joys and sorrows.

And then when the time comes, He will give us what is beyond fair.

So even though I may be more than a half century old and yet have much to learn—no worries! I have my whole life ahead of me. Today I am making choices. I choose to increase the number of times I rejoice at my blessings and smile while I clean up my crumbly messes. I have decided to learn from them and to trust that God is in them, with His higher purpose. I am baking a lot of cookies these days. Chocolate chip anyone?

*Today, if you hear his voice,
do not harden your hearts.*
Hebrews 3:15

Chapter 6

Wet bread

Humor in life is like seasoning on our stuffing; without it, we just have wet bread.

Let the trees of the forest sing,
Let them sing for joy before the LORD.
1 Chronicles 16:33

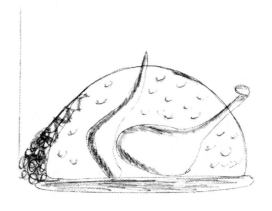

I SLIDE MY HAND OUT FROM UNDER the covers in the darkness. Slowly, so as not to wake my husband from his heavy sleep. I reach for the pen and notepad on the nightstand. A tiny click announces the pen is cocked. It glows with a faint purple-white light. My husband presented this lighted pen to me as a gift for just such late-night authoring.

He awakens now and asks, "What are you doing?"

"Nothing."

He repeats: "What are you doing?"

"Just writing."

"About what?"

"Humor," I squeak.

"OK, Honey."

He doesn't question the subject matter, or even the fact that I am writing it at 2 a.m. He simply rolls over and goes back to sleep.

Ugh! He doesn't find it strange that I am writing notes about "humor" in the middle of the night? What's wrong with him? What's wrong with me? Why isn't this funny? Maybe this is serious. It could be serious. Of course it's serious. I'm always serious when I use humor. Unless, of course, I'm not. What I mean to say is: Just the fact that I may be using humor in any given situation doesn't automatically indicate that I'm not serious.

Life is serious, isn't it? Serious enough that a sense of humor can be a very valuable relief. It can help bring refreshment to the daily staleness that can creep in unnoticed. Or it can even bring relief from the pain we suffer. Where there is pain, there is growth. It's true. But, where there is humor, there is tolerance of the pain and acceptance, even joy, in the growth.

Humor brings a more tranquil understanding of the difficult lessons put before us. Lessons we might otherwise miss because we find ourselves half asleep, not fully paying attention to the mundane experience of our day. Humor gives us a different perspective. We see events through a bright new lens. It can help us swallow things that may otherwise leave a bitter taste in our mouths.

I was a hospice volunteer for many years and spent countless hours talking with people who were facing the end of their days here on earth. Many of those days were filled with pain and physical limitations that could dishearten the best of us.

I was always humbly amazed by those people who could stop in the middle of being sad and just laugh! Laugh at themselves, at life. Even laugh at the horrible disease they battled. They seemed to be recharged from the time spent looking at the silly side of sadness.

They knew God had a bigger plan and that their pain was not forever. God had blessed them with the ability to find joy in all circumstances, and I have had the benefit of learning from them about how important it is to embrace that joy. Indeed, even seek it out from under the heavy cloak where it hides.

Humor gives us a new dimension. Makes curves out of an otherwise flat journey. It colors our world in shades and hues that delight our senses. It unburdens our heart and lightens our load. With humor, we are better able to walk in another's shoes. Understand their perspective without becoming defensive.

With the help humor offers, we can recreate ourselves, become better people. We can laugh at our own weaknesses. If we are more relaxed about our weakness, we can look it in the face and improve upon it. Humor helps us to acknowledge a difficult situation, therefore taking away some of its power and transferring that power back to ourselves.

Humor is love; humor is grace; humor is strength. Humor is one of our precious God-given gifts. Ask God to help you share a smile today. Maybe, even a belly laugh.

One day, my granddaughter was pouting about something her brother did. "Don't pout, Honey," I instructed. "It will ruin your whole day."

"Oh no!" she quipped. "I've done this before and my day was just fine." Ahh yes!

What is in your oven of life? Are you roasting stuffing, seasoned generously with humor, or are you just baking wet bread?

*Today, if you hear his voice,
do not harden your hearts.*
Hebrews 3:15

Chapter 7

Perfectly imperfect

Adam named his wife Eve, because she would become the mother of all the living.
Genesis 3:20

Vinegar tastes great on hash browns

"The Lord God said, 'It is not good for the man to be alone.
I will make a helper suitable for him.'"
Genesis 2:18

MY HUSBAND LOVES VINEGAR ON HASH browns. This triggers the gag reflex in me. Why would anyone want crisp hash browns, just to sog them up with vinegar? He has been the recipient of many blank stares from reluctant waiters. "Excuse me, sir, you said 'vinegar'? Yes sir; right away, sir." How could this man eat so differently from me? How could he be so different from me? Welcome to the union of marriage!

Many times our thinking limits our wisdom. We tend to think inside our own "experience box," and like passing gas under the covers, it has no place to go.

Such was the case with me and marriage. My mind, resting inside this limited experience box, became increasingly stupid. Making the same comfortable mistakes. Unable to see any more than the four corners. Indeed! Marriage is one situation where we all need to use some uncommon sense. Someone once told me that the heart is forever foolish. This takes me back to a song from the 60s by Judy Collins: "It's love's illusions I recall; I really don't know love at all."

I grew up with no marriage example. My parents divorced when I was five. I didn't have the opportunity to witness the give-and-take that happens in a healthy marriage. I am not, however, one to blame everything on my childhood. I believe in taking responsibility for myself, my actions, and their consequences. I have no one but myself to blame. I believe this—probably to a fault.

You see, I like to drive. I mean, I *really* like to drive. I've never been a really good copilot. I get bored adjusting the temperature controls. No, I prefer to drive. I committed myself early on to being self-reliant and self-protecting, refusing to depend on someone else to meet my needs—material, social, spiritual, or otherwise. But we were not created to live that way. We are a social race. In marriage, this degree of self-sufficiency becomes the enemy. It works against the union, rather than for it.

However, a dependence on your marriage partner for everything can be just as lethal. Depending on your spouse to give you all the love you could ever use, or all the social support necessary to sustain you, is unrealistic. No one can ever sustain you like God. As a husband and wife, you are an imperfect team. You will slip and slide in the vinegar of marriage. We need God to maintain a healthy union.

I went through two marriages before I understood this. Something I am not proud of. My base was overcome because I didn't have a solid one. I am far from the expert, but God is. Rely on Him. I asked Christ to come into my life at the age of twelve, and He did. For many years into adulthood, I treated Him like the hired help, not a valued houseguest, but He did something funny: He went outside and rang the doorbell.

I came to know that He was my greatest resource and trusted friend in all things. I started out thinking that I shouldn't bother Him about every issue. Surprise! He wants an "every day, every way" kind of relationship. He doesn't want to be like an emergency room physician, who rushes in at the last minute to resuscitate a broken marriage. Although He could. We can't change where we have been, but we can change where we are going. In God, all things are possible.

"That is why a man leaves his father and mother and is united to his wife, and they become one flesh" (Genesis 2:24).

It was God's intention to create man and woman differently. Let us celebrate those differences. With Him, all is reconciled beautifully.

Now, each morning, I happily set the breakfast table with vinegar. I don't put vinegar on hash browns for myself. That would be a stretch. I have, however, found a great many uses for it. Here are a few:

1. For a sore throat, gargle with vinegar. It is a natural antibiotic.

2. Use it on your skin as an antiseptic. It kills germs.

3. Pat it on beestings to relieve the pain.

Mothers-in-law are not puppies.

Who is wise and understanding among you?
Let them show it by their good life, by deeds
done in the humility that comes from wisdom.
James 3:13

"**T**UNE IN, TURN ON, DROP OUT.**"** If you remember this phrase, you may be a baby boomer. You may also find yourself caring for elderly parents or in-laws. What a difference a half-century makes, huh!

Have you walked through a nursing home lately? There are a lot of sad and broken people there. Have you ever tried to visualize yourself as one of them? How would you feel? I have had better visions. My husband and I wanted something better for my mother-in-law, so we brought her home to live with us. Boy! Did I have a huge learning curve. It wasn't like bringing home a puppy! She was kinda cute, but that was where the similarities ended.

I wish I could say it was easy and every day was a blessing, but that is not how it felt. Dementia was painful to watch and slow to consume her. And sometimes it seemed as though I was going with her. We have already talked about how important the use of humor is and I thank God for it. Thank you, thank you, thank you. Amen.

Such go the next twelve years:

My mother-in-law had her own rooms inside our home. They were some distance from the main living quarters. She also had her own phone with a private number. One afternoon, she was getting ready to go to the doctor. I was her transportation. "Just use your phone to call me when you're ready," I told her since that method is much easier than trying to yell.

"OK," she agreed.

Minutes went by and it was nearing time to go. No call came. I went to check on her and found her sitting in her recliner, coat on, her purse in her lap.

"Why didn't you call?" I asked.

"Oh! I didn't think of it," she replied.

Her strength and balance were lessening, so I cleaned her rooms each week. I would get down on my hands and knees to check the floor for the ongoing parade of objects that she had dropped. I would find anything from spilled coffee, to bobby pins, note cards, tissues, stool softeners, chocolate raisins, and unidentifiable objects of concern. For this work, I do not wear my finest clothes.

One particular day, she had me looking for an earring that she lost. I crawled around on the floor for quite some time and was overjoyed to have found it. I stood up and exclaimed, "Look, I found it!"

"Don't you have any better jeans to wear than those? You look like something the cat dragged in," was her only reply.

When she began to forget things, we had to make sure she took her medications. I would set them out for her to take with each meal. One day, I went in to check if she had taken her pills after lunch. She usually ate lunch at 11:30 and it was now 1p.m.

"You haven't taken your lunchtime pills yet," I remarked.

"That is because I haven't had lunch yet," she replied.

"It is 1 o'clock. Aren't you hungry?" I asked.

"No, I just had lunch," she quipped.

This conversation is like none I'd ever had before; yet lately, it was strangely familiar.

We had a much-needed and rare vacation planned. We were planning to go to Hawaii. The anticipation was delicious. I could hardly wait. Two days before takeoff, Mom fell and fractured her hip. *Vacation cancelled; surgery scheduled; therapy in our future.*

Another time we took a short trip to the Coast for a few days of rest. We received a call from Mom on the second morning. She claimed she couldn't get out of bed. "Come home," she pled.

"What do you mean you can't get out of bed, Mom?" Do you mean that your arthritis is flaring and it's difficult to get out of bed?"

"No I can't get out of bed."

"Are you in pain anywhere?"

"No, I just can't get out of bed."

We thought that perhaps she'd had a stroke. We were an hour away from home and make it in about forty-five minutes. When we walked in the door, she was making tea at the stove. When we questioned her, she replied, "Well, I didn't mean literally!"

Sometimes the best thing to say is nothing at all.

She loved peaches. She ate them on cottage cheese. We would be asked to scour all the fruit stands in the area to find the first available peaches of the season. One year, she was having a difficult time waiting for the first picking. "I need peaches now!" she demanded.

"Mom, we have looked, and they tell us the very first peaches may be ripe for picking in a few days—if the sun holds. We will go and buy some cottage cheese and then the minute they're ready, you will be also."

"Don't buy me cottage cheese! I don't want it if you won't get me peaches."

Food issues were big. She would have us buy her the same foods over and over each week. When we realized she wasn't eating them, but simply storing them—and running out of space to do it—we had to explain that we would not buy more until she ate some of what she already had. We showed her that they would expire and need to be thrown out, if not eaten.

"No, I need more!"

"Why?"

"Because I'm frugal."

Exasperated, we'd reply, "Mom, it's only frugal if you actually use it."

Bathing her was difficult because she had an extreme

fear of water. At that point, I had a fear of myself when bathing her. I feared that my patience would run out.

I wasn't even sure I liked her, but God loved her and asked us to do the same. I could not have done this without His grace. He gave me strength for each new day. I'd ask for a more grateful and serving heart and He would provide.

He never asks us for more than we can give, and after twelve years, when she began to walk out the door at night, we knew we could no longer provide for her in the same way. God, however, continues to provide.

At the time of this writing, she is ninety-six years old and in a nursing home. By His grace, she is reasonably happy. We see her each day and sometimes she knows who we are. Caring for an elderly family member in your home is not like caring for a puppy. It is 24/7— 365 days a year. Consider it. Pray over it. Then if you feel called to do it,-bless you and serve well, my friend. Serve well. For it is God you are serving.

It was funny and frustrating. Serious and silly. I thank God for the experience. Looking back, He taught me well.

You may think this is a sad story, and some aspects of it are. But God in His mercy gives us grace and humor in the midst of trial. Just the other day she said, "I can't seem to remember much anymore, and it worries me. I don't want to live in a nursing home." Indeed!

PART C

Grandma's "not-to-do" list

Truly I tell you, unless you change and become like little children, you will never enter the kingdom of heaven.
Matthew 18:3

MOTHER'S HAVE "TO-DO" LISTS. THEY ARE necessary and they are important. As mothers we cannot be just friends to our kids. We must be authoritative. Mothers and fathers must teach values and responsibility. Direction and compassion. How to put the toilet seat down and why you can't put beans in your little brother's ears. This is hard work and a big commitment that God has entrusted to us.

Grandmas have "not-to-do" lists. Now, don't get your shorts in a tangle! Grandparents should never forget the influence they have on their grandkids. It also is our responsibility to play a big role in raising up children of God. We are to be good examples. We are second in command to their parents.

What I want to talk about here, however, are the unique blessings given to grandmas. Time, and a little hind end'sight. Time to play; and when the kids go home, time to rest. Time to bake cookies, time to rest. Time to set up a tent fort, time to rest. Time to think about our "not-to-do" lists. Below, are some items on my list:

1. **Not to take myself so seriously.** Do I always need to be the perfect teacher or is OK to conduct a belching contest?

2. **Not to worry that others might be better at this than myself.** As a young mother, I sometimes thought that if I was charming, maybe no one would notice how defective I was at this. Now, I think, *Perhaps, because I'm slightly defective, everyone will think I'm charming.* Because, let's face it, we're all defective. Join the club!

3. **Not to use my energy on the small stuff.** Things get knocked over—keep playing!

4. **Not to let a cherished moment slip away.** When my oldest granddaughter was small, I asked her if

she knew what her address was. "Yes," she replied. "I have a pink dress, and a red dress, and a blue dress." Very good!

5. **Not to use punishment when a good story could teach the same lesson.** Punishment has its place, but a lesson taught with humor and love is learned more effectively than a lesson taught with anger.

As a grandma, I no longer feel the need to create an illusion that I know it all. Besides, I have an excuse. The kids may just think I am getting a bit senile.

I have heard it said, "I'm not old; I've just been young for a very long time." That is the grandma I want to be.

I love being called Grandma and to contemplate questions like:

What if people could fly?

Do dinosaurs like cookies?

How far away is Heaven?

P. S.

My grandpa sold me his 1957 Chevy for one dollar. I never thanked him properly. He is with the Lord now. Thank you, from the bottom of my heart, Grandpa. Thank you.

My Little Boy Was Leaving

God sent a precious babe to me so many years ago.
A young mother in awe of what I held in my arms,
back then I could not know
what I thought was mine to keep forever,
to mold and shape as I pleased.
From the very beginning, from close in my arms,
my little boy was leaving.

Every venture and each new step must have been a clue
that this little bird would fly from the nest
to conquer world's anew.
Like the butterfly and the sparrow,
like the salmon in the stream,
in God and nature's unique plan,
each goes forth to find his dream.

From frogs and worms, to girls and cars,
the years—where did they go?
My babe in arms has grown so tall,
and oh, how I love him so.
How proud I am of this young man
who stands before me today,
and I wonder, would I have been so brave
If I had known
my little boy was leaving.

Cathy Nelson
1990

Today, *if you hear his voice, do not harden your hearts.*
Hebrews 3:15

Chapter 8

Mary, Mary, how does your garden grow?

The LORD will guide you always;
he will satisfy your needs in a sun-scorched land
and will strengthen your frame.
You will be like a well-watered garden,
like a spring whose waters never fail.
Isaiah 58:11

Cathy Nelson

THE BITING WINDS OF WINTER HAVE mellowed to the soft warm breezes of spring. It plays in my hair and kisses my cheek. God's faithful work done in the dark of winter is revealed once again as hundreds of tiny buds burst forth into a rainbow of color. I kneel down in the rich soil, nearly hidden among the tall flowers. To spot me would be like working one of those hidden picture puzzles. The sweet fragrances fill my senses. Lavender, daphne, honeysuckle, and lilac.

Out of the rich brown earth life springs abundant. I can almost feel the flowers breathe in and out, softly against me. They are alive. Swarms of honeybees move contented from color to color. They ignore my presence, so focused on their work. The sun warms my back. My hands, ungloved, move the rich soil around the base of my newest planting. The soil's meaty fragrance complements the sweetness of the flowers. A fat earthworm slides away from me.

I love to garden. To witness the ongoing miracle of life. Working in a hospital setting with very ill patients can at times empty me. Working in a living, growing garden fills me anew. Tending to the growing plants feeds my soul, yet it humbles me. I could not begin to create such beauty. I come to know true humility surrounded by God's amazing attention to detail. Thousands of intricate, tiny details. All His design.

One ounce of healthy soil can contain billions of tiny beneficial bacteria. These soil microbes produce life. They are necessary for the mineralization of elements that sustain plant health. But the many microbes must be in correct balance. They need oxygen, water, and light in order to flourish and do their work. The flowers need the microbes to thrive—not only in the spring, but throughout the growing season and even into the dormant time of winter.

Humans also have a need for ongoing nourishment. Food, water, sunlight, and the Living Word. We cannot expect to thrive from one reading. To flourish we must be immersed in His Word from season to season. We have short memories. We need to remember what we already know. We have a big thirst that only God can quench. We need the water of life.

Jesus said, **"Everyone who drinks this water will be thirsty again, but whoever drinks the water I give them will never thirst"** (John 4:13–14).

All the answers to life's struggles are found in the Bible; we only need to spend time with it. Developing the habit of turning to His Word in good times will better ensure that we will turn to it in bad times—and for a lifetime. Keep it open.

A flower's beauty is more than appearances. We enjoy its loveliness, but without the good soil to sustain it, we have no flower. We, too, need good soil to sustain us.

"The seed falling on rocky ground refers to someone who hears the word and at once receives it with joy. But since they have no root, they last only a short time. When trouble or persecution comes because of the word, they quickly fall away. The seed falling among the thorns refers to someone who hears the word, but the worries of this life and the deceitfulness of wealth choke the word, making it unfruitful. But the seed falling on good soil refers to someone who hears the word and understands it. This is the one who produces a crop, yielding a hundred, sixty or thirty times what was sown" (Matthew 13:20–23).

We need time to allow God's Word to settle into our minds and come to thrive there. Protected by the shelter of His arms, I will continue to grow. Here, in the quiet of my garden I see God's beauty, feel His renewing joy, and hear His steady whisper.

We can learn so much when we listen more and talk less.

One evening, my son had put his three younger boys to bed and he could hear them talking at a late hour. He went in and asked them to stop talking and go to sleep. The smallest quipped, "But, Dad, I have only been doing 1% of the conversation!" Maybe he has something there. Maybe we should all be doing 1% of the conversation and listening much more.

Today, if you hear his voice,
do not harden your hearts.
Hebrews 3:15

Chapter 9

What would Lassie do?

The wolf will live with the lamb,
the leopard will lie down with the goat,
the calf and the lion and the yearling together;
and a little child will lead them.
Isaiah 11:6

WHY DO YOU SUPPOSE GOD MADE dogs? *So we could clean nose juice off car windows and fur balls off carpets?* Nah! I don't think so. We are only willing to do these chores in exchange for payment far richer. I think God made dogs for a very noble reason.

Jesus was expert at teaching us through the use of parables. Parables are brief stories using physical symbols to illustrate a spiritual truth. I think God created the dog as a modern-day parable—a parable to teach us about faithfulness and forgiveness in a wise and gentle way.

In the book of Matthew we find many parables. In the parable of the mustard seed, Jesus said that the kingdom of heaven is like a mustard seed. Though it is the smallest seed, when it grows it becomes a tree. He said this to explain how even though the kingdom has small beginnings, with faithfulness on our part, it will grow and produce everlasting results.

In the parable of the unforgiving debtor, the master forgave the servant for the debt that was owed him, but then the servant turned around and threatened one of his fellow servants over a small debt he himself was owed. When the master heard of the servant's actions, it angered him, and he turned the servant over to the jailers to be tortured. It teaches that we cannot be faithful to God if we are not as forgiving of others as God is forgiving toward us.

Faithfulness and forgiveness are required of us when we are following after God. Our furry friends teach us faithfulness. They never give up on us; they are faithful through and through. Always by our side, a sure friend. They teach us forgiveness. They never judge us and are always forgiving even when we neglect to feed them dinner on time. They remain firmly devoted to us even though we are quite flawed. How much easier should it be for us to remain faithful to an absolutely perfect God?

I have learned something valuable from every dog I've ever owned. My childhood dog was most forgiving. My siblings and I did not always treat her with the utmost care. She was a very small toy terrier and everything we ever did to her could not have been comfortable, but she always forgave us, and when I was blue over something, she was my most trusted confident.

As a young adult, I had a small black spaniel mix. We sold her when we were preparing to move out of state. She found her way several miles to my grandfather's house, where she must have picked up my scent because she would not leave. He called to inform me that she had been there for hours. Faithful through adversity!

Later in my life, a large sheepdog prevented a less than reputable man from entering my front door. Protector, faithful!

An intelligent corgi, who went outside with me to greet several family members arriving at our home for a holiday gathering, found himself locked out for a long period of time until someone noticed he wasn't underfoot. When we discovered our error, there he sat on the front porch, waiting. Faithful and always willing to obey.

An Australian shepherd, who looks square into my face for every mood or reaction, so she can react in kind. Faithful, serving.

From the first time they raise their paws for a handshake to the tail wagging end, our dogs are a parable of what faithful should look like. The Lord, once again in His cleverness, planned well.

Exercise your faithfulness. Take your dog for a walk and while you're out there, pray about all the ways you can be more faithful and forgiving to friends and family. Let's ask the Lord to pour His faithfulness into us. His payment is rich.

"They will wage war against the Lamb, but the Lamb will triumph over them because He is Lord of lords and King of kings—and with him will be his called, chosen and *faithful* followers" (Revelation 17:14).

Today, if you hear his voice,
do not harden your hearts.
Hebrews 3:15

Chapter 10

Accumulated hind end'sight

They will still bear fruit in old age,
they will stay fresh and green, proclaiming,
"The Lord is upright."
Psalm 92:14–15

W HEN I WAS A CHILD, I would make up stories for my younger sisters. Each time I would hold the very same book in my hands, but I would see a different story and share that story with them. Now, as adults, they tell me that they delighted in this.

As I work through the second half of my life, I relish the idea that I can continue to change my story. I know that with God, I'm an ever-evolving good work in progress.

"Being confident of this, that he who began a good work in you will carry it on to completion until the day of Christ Jesus" (Philippians 1:6).

My story is not yet over. I have learned much along the way, but the anticipation of the fruit from tomorrow's hind end'sight stirs me. Though far from expert, if I listen to what God has to say to me and let it guide the learning I have yet to do, I will be enriched from the experience.

The journey of self-discovery with God is timeless. Some of us reach retirement, weighed down with a feeling that "this may be all there is, and then we die." I believe this is our soul longing for what it naturally knows is something better. Urging us to fix our compass on true north. To lessen our grip on things of no value in this world. God may ask us for more of our time now. He asks us to hold on to what is right and true for the rest of the journey and to begin to release all the weighty clutter that we have accumulated in our youth. I rejoice in the lighter load. His grace will lead me home.

It is time to question our intentions. Am I doing this task because I want to impress others or because God is calling me to it? What is our main reference point? In what direction is our story headed? What does the world see when they look at our Christian walk? What one word would they use to describe us? Fearful, angry, joyless? It is time to shatter our hardened hearts and pause to remember that what we have to share with the world really is *good news.*

I have made my share of mistakes in life. If you have also, join me in changing your story. I pray that God will help us ripen rather than rot on the vine. I wish to recognize the joy of having less and to understand that youth lies in appreciation of what I do have.

I want to wake up and smell the marshmallows. I want God to train my eyes to see the treasure long before the end of the rainbow. I want to notice purple mountain majesties, warm sunshine through a winter window, and crisp red apples. I want to let go so I can hold on. I want to truly love, and I want to be very, very contagious.

At eighteen, I knew everything. At thirty, I revisited. At forty, started over. Now, the truth is: I don't have all the answers, but I expect to have many more of them, just as soon as I have accumulated more hind end'sight. And, I thank God. He hasn't given me everything I've asked for.

One of my grandsons said something very special that was not typical of the eight-year-old he is. When his siblings made fun of him for something he did, he responded in an uncharacteristic calm" "Well! I'm only eight, ya know!" adding "That is not even a decade old."

Already, wisdom is forming.

If I have decades left, I pray that I will use them well and wisely. With God's help I can reinvent and improve on the story I call "self." So my story lives on, pursuing the peace— a place where God speaks—over all the rituals I have been living by, and it impacts my story more than anything else ever will.

If you would like to change your story, let Him rewrite it. Give Him your pen. Change your shirt, change your story, move forward. Keep Him in the center of your story. You need not be an expert. It doesn't take anything heroic. Just don't be late when He calls *for all of hope is in His call*. And do believe in happy endings.

Martin Luther wrote: "If you could understand a single grain of wheat you would die of wonder." When my story on earth is over, I want to die of wonder, looking into His face and know the author of all life.

Today, if you hear his voice,
do not harden your hearts.
Hebrews 3:15